Benjamin Harrison

Ritual Uniformity and Elasticity, and Church Desecration

A charge, delivered to the clergy of the Archdeaconry of Maidstone, at the

ordinary visitation in April and May, MDCCCLXXIII

Benjamin Harrison

Ritual Uniformity and Elasticity, and Church Desecration
A charge, delivered to the clergy of the Archdeaconry of Maidstone, at the ordinary visitation in April and May, MDCCCLXXIII

ISBN/EAN: 9783337426316

Printed in Europe, USA, Canada, Australia, Japan

Cover: Foto ©Lupo / pixelio.de

More available books at **www.hansebooks.com**

Ritual Uniformity and Elasticity, and Church Desecration

A CHARGE

DELIVERED TO THE

CLERGY OF THE ARCHDEACONRY OF MAIDSTONE,

At the Ordinary Visitation

IN APRIL AND MAY, MDCCCLXXIII.

BY

BENJAMIN HARRISON, M.A.

ARCHDEACON OF MAIDSTONE

London

RIVINGTONS, WATERLOO PLACE

HIGH STREET | TRINITY STREET
Oxford | Cambridge

CANTERBURY; A. GINDER, ST. GEORGE'S HALL; HAL DRURY, MERCERY LANE; MAIDSTONE, WICKHAM AND SON.

1873

TO THE REVEREND THE

RURAL DEANS AND CLERGY

OF THE

ARCHDEACONRY OF MAIDSTONE;

AND TO

THEIR LAY BRETHREN, THE CHURCHWARDENS AND SIDESMEN,

ASSEMBLED WITH THEM IN VISITATION ;

WHO WERE PLEASED TO REQUEST THE PUBLICATION,

This Charge

IS NOW

Inscribed

WITH EVERY SENTIMENT OF RESPECTFUL AND AFFECTIONATE REGARD.

PRECINCTS, CANTERBURY,
JUNE VI., MDCCCLXXIII.

A CHARGE

My Reverend Brethren,

We are again met together, through God's good providence, with our lay brethren who are associated with you in Church offices, in this our solemn yearly assembly. Last autumn we had the satisfaction of seeing amongst us, for the first time, in the exercise of the Visitatorial function, our Most Reverend Diocesan, after an interval of twice the usual period in this Diocese for the holding of the Archbishop's Visitation. His revered Predecessor, as his Grace reminded you in the opening of his first Address delivered at Maidstone, was on the point of holding his Second Visitation, and had, as you well know, partly written his Charge, when he was taken from us to his rest; and the serious illness of his Successor, before the first year of his office was completed, deferred for another three years the customary Visitation of the Diocese.

The inquiries which the Archbishop issued to his

Clergy, and the answers to which were given in at
the Visitation, were, as I need not say to you, very
full and precise, and the returns thus made are now
undergoing, in due order, his Grace's careful examination ; his attention being directed, as many of
you doubtless are aware, not only to any deficiencies
to be supplied, or things faulty to be corrected,
but also to anything which appeared worthy of
special notice in the way of commendation.[1] The
presentments made by the Churchwardens have
been followed up in like manner, on his Grace's
part, by due inquiry ; and have either been dealt
with directly by the Archbishop himself, or referred
by him, where it seemed convenient, to the subor-
dinate officer, or authority, to whom it appeared
specially to belong. I may add, with particular
reference to the fabrics and fittings of the churches,
which it is the Archdeacon's duty, in a special sense,
to look after, that the week's visit which the Archbishop paid at Maidstone, staying at the Mote,
while he held an Ordination also in All Saints'
Church on the Sunday, having on the Friday consecrated the new Church of St. Faith, afforded his
Grace an opportunity, of which he fully availed
himself, of personally inspecting several of the
churches in the neighbouring villages, and in some

---

[1] As in one instance, which came incidentally to my knowledge, in
which, as the result of the returns given in, particular inquiry was made
in regard to the means by which a great increase had been obtained in
the number of communicants.

of the outlying places within reach. I believe I
am warranted in saying—and I report it with much
satisfaction,—that the Archbishop, in the course of
these casual visits, found tokens, beyond what he
had expected, of cost and care bestowed in the restoration of the fabrics, and in the increased accommodation, or improved arrangements made in them
for Divine Service. "No one can go," said his
Grace—in his Address delivered at Maidstone on
the first day of his Visitation, "no one can go,—as
I have been going during the last few days, from
church to church in this neighbourhood, without
being struck with the great improvement which
has taken place in the condition of the Houses of
God." "There is much more of that seemly ap-
pearance which we desire to see in the House of
God—much more accommodation for the poor."

"This I consider," said the Archbishop, "to be
greatly owing to the Diocesan Society" — the
Diocesan Church Building and Endowment Society;
which he therefore earnestly commended to the
Clergy and Laity assembled at the Visitation;
anxious to carry on effectually, by its aid, the work
which his honoured Predecessor had so much at
heart, and which he had set on foot at the cost of
great personal exertion, and with success correspond-
ing with his efforts. Desiring as I do to further,
to the utmost of my power, the earnest recommendation herein of our Diocesan, especially to those of
our lay brethren possessed of worldly means, who

have come into the Diocese since the Society was
first established, and who occupy, in many in-
stances, important places within its borders, I
feel at the same time that I am only fulfilling a
duty, and paying a debt, in acknowledging that it
is a "gift" which has been, now through a period
of many years, " bestowed upon us by the means of
many persons," for which thanks are to be "given
by many on our behalf."[1] Looking back, not only
to the period when it first became my official duty
to give my care and attention to this object, but
further back than this, to the time—now well-nigh
thirty-five years ago—when, in attendance upon
Archbishop Howley in his circuits of confirmation,
and on other occasions, I first became acquainted
with the churches of the Diocese, I cannot but
recognize gratefully how much is owing to the
valuable services of a body of men whose office
the Archbishop had revived in the Diocese—I need
not say I mean the Rural Deans—greatly to the
assistance of the Diocesan and of the Archdeacon,
by their frequent visits of inspection and their
friendly counsel always at hand. I feel, also, how
greatly we are indebted to the zeal and charity of
the parochial Clergy, and I ought to add, also, in
many cases specially, of their wives and families;
"for to their power, I bear them record, yea, and
beyond their power, they have been ready of
themselves"[2] in this good work, involving much

[1] 2 Cor. i. 11.   [2] 2 Cor. viii. 2.

self-denying sacrifice and active exertion, and oftentimes patient waiting for the fulfilment of a long-cherished desire and hope. And last, but not least, I must express how much we owe to the cordial co-operation of their lay brethren, the Churchwardens, and with them, and often by their means, to a great extent, of the body of Churchmen in their several parishes, and other friends.

The work is happily still going on. Since I last addressed you, church restoration,—external repair and internal improvement,—has been in hand, and is now completed, in the churches of Downe, Eastchurch, Milstead, Offham, Orpington, Ryarsh, and Sittingbourne. Re-arrangement of seats, with great improvement of the interior, has been effected in the Church of Bromley; and external repair has been taken in hand at Bethersden, re-arrangement within having been made some years ago. The completion of Trinity Church, Sittingbourne, in a very populous and growing neighbourhood, is now going forward. Similar works have been undertaken, or are contemplated, at Eynesford, Capel, Tudeley, and Hollingbourne. The church at Speldhurst has been replaced by a new and beautiful fabric; a like work is in progress at Bexley Heath; a new church is now building at Murston, far more conveniently situated than the old church for the parishioners, greatly multiplied, as they have been of late years, by the brick-fields; and a church has been erected on

Charing Heath, which will be a witness and memorial of individual zeal and liberality, as well as a great benefit to an outlying and scattered population. In the principal town of the Archdeaconry an important work has been accomplished in the revival of St. Faith's Church, with its parochial machinery about it; the new church having been consecrated by the Archbishop at the time of his Visitation, as I have said, in September last. And I trust that the arrangements which are now in hand, and which have for some time been a matter of some anxiety and careful communication between the several parties concerned, may successfully overcome the difficulties by which it has been beset, and result in the building of a new church, and the more complete organization of the district, in the West Borough of Maidstone; carrying on and completing, in a neighbourhood where building has of late been going on to a great extent, the work which, more than thirty years ago, was happily begun, by the recovery and enlargement, after a long period of desecration, of the ancient "Pilgrims' Chapel," the present Church of St. Peter's. I must also mention, with satisfaction and thankfulness, the completion and consecration last summer of the new Church of St. Paul's, Sheerness, and the encouraging progress of the mission and pastoral work in that place.

In connection with these matters, I must advert to the labours of a Committee of Convocation now

sitting, appointed " to consider what deficiencies
exist in the amount of spiritual ministrations provided by the Church of England for the people of
England and Wales, and the means by which these
wants may best be supplied." The Committee,
feeling that they should in that way most effectually
and regularly obtain the information they desired,
requested the Archdeacons of the Province to
forward the inquiries which the Committee had
drawn up, to the Clergy, in particular, of populous
parishes in their several Archdeaconries. I felt
somewhat unwilling to inflict upon the Clergy of
my own Archdeaconry, who had so lately been
called upon for such full and accurate returns to be
made to their Diocesan on the occasion of his
primary Visitation, any additional labour of this
kind. The object in view, however, appeared very
important, and the action of the Committee of
Convocation highly desirable; and I have to make
my acknowledgments to my brethren of the Clergy
for the readiness with which they met the application made to them, and the careful and painstaking
manner in which they supplied, very promptly, the
information desired.

At my last Visitation I intimated my intention
of entering, in the course of the summer, on a
parochial Visitation—the fourth which I shall
have made, when completed—of the churches
throughout the Archdeaconry. I visited, accordingly, in that summer, the deaneries of Sutton and

Sittingbourne, and hoped last year to have gone
round the other deaneries before the Archbishop's
Visitation. I was able to visit the Western Division of the deanery of Charing, and some few of
the parishes in the Eastern Division, and also in the
Northern and Southern Divisions of the deanery of
Malling : but the illness at the time of two of my
brethren, the Rural Deans, prevented my visiting
their deaneries ; and then the customary inhibition,
pending the Archbishop's approaching Visitation,
put an end to my further progress. I hope, however, in the course of the present summer, to complete the parochial Visitation of these deaneries,
and to visit the deaneries also of Croydon, Dartford,
and Shoreham. The anticipations which I had
expressed to you, at my last Visitation two years
ago, in regard to the progress which had been made
since last I went my rounds, were, I am happy to
say, fully borne out : there was little to note in the
way of defects to be supplied, or things amiss to be
corrected, compared with the improvements to be
recorded with satisfaction and thankfulness, works
of zeal and love, " for the house of our God, and for
the offices thereof,"[1] to be highly commended and
approved. While speaking of the several Ruridecanal Divisions, I may mention that the Archbishop has seen fit to subdivide further what was
lately called the deanery of Dartford, divided as it
had been some years ago into the Eastern and

---

[1] Neh. xiii. 14.

Western Divisions. The further subdivision now made will revive very advantageously, and to the restoration of an old title, the deanery of Croydon, which will comprise the whole of that original parish, with Addington, and the adjoining parish of West Wickham. The extensive deanery of Bridge, in the Archdeaconry of Canterbury, having been in like manner divided into East and West, the entire Diocese will now contain twenty Rural-deaneries, ten in each Archdeaconry.

In speaking, when I last addressed you, of the distinctive character of these Visitation Courts and Synods, of their original constitution, and the purposes they had been designed, or in the course of time made, to serve, looking back through their past history, and having regard to their present use, I took occasion to notice the opportunity which they had afforded of making known, officially, and in due Ecclesiastical order, to the Clergy, and to the Laity with them, in their several local divisions, the legislative measures,—the Canons and Orders or Statutes—which had been passed in provincial Synods and Convocations, or enacted by the national Legislature, in the combined action of the Church and the State. It may be regarded as in conformity with this general principle, or practice, that our most Reverend Diocesan pointed out, explicitly, in one of his Visitation Addresses, the provisions which, having been first approved by Convocation, had been "embodied in a Bill and laid before Parliament, and in the course of the last session passed into a law; giving to the Clergy increased liberty in their ministrations, as regulated by the law of Church and State, to meet the religious wants of the people, amidst the new circumstances and multiplied exigencies of the present time." And not only so, but his Grace took care further to append to his published Charge a detailed statement of the provisions contained in the "Act of Uniformity Amendment Act," as it is termed, of the last session.[1] The Archbishop was desirous not only of showing to how great an extent the Church practically possessed the power, notwithstanding her relations with the State, of adapting her Services to the wants of her children, but also of impressing upon his Clergy "the duty of carefully considering," as he said, "in their several spheres, how far it was desirable that they should avail themselves of the liberty thus given; in particular, how, inasmuch as the law which had recently passed had enabled the Clergy to accommodate the daily Services to the wants of the people," "every clergyman," he thought, would "be naturally expected to consider carefully, in his parish, how far this new system opens to him opportunities of Common Prayer which were denied to him before."

It seems to me important, my Reverend Bre-

[1] Act 35 & 36 Vict. chap. 35.

thren, to recall to your recollection these state-
ments and exhortations of the Archbishop, as well
that they may not fail of their practical effect, as
also with a view to guard the legislative provisions
in question from misapprehensions to which, I
think, they have been in some quarters exposed.
As regards "the Shortened Order for Morning
Prayer or for Evening Prayer, specified in the
schedule to the Act,"—I use the words of the
Archbishop's summary—"which Order may, on
any day except Sunday, Christmas Day, Ash
Wednesday, Good Friday, and Ascension Day, be
used, if in a cathedral, in addition to, and if in a
church, in lieu of, the Order for Morning or for
Evening Prayer, respectively prescribed by the
Book of Common Prayer," it is right that we
should bear distinctly in mind the precise object
for which this provision has been made. It has
been because, in his Grace's words, "no one can
doubt that there are in all town parishes, and often
in country parishes, persons to whom it is a great
blessing to have daily access to their parish church,
in order that they may invoke God's blessing
on the labours of the day;" while, on the other
hand, " experience has shown how difficult it is to
gather together any large congregation of hearty
worshippers in the midst of the busy occupations
of men's lives in this age." And, undoubtedly, it
is most gratifying and encouraging to find how
many, especially in the season of Lent lately past,

amidst the full tide of business in the metropolis, have been found to avail themselves of the opportunity of attending a short Service, of a quarter of an hour or so, in the middle of the day. Only it must be borne in mind at the same time that, while the wants of persons so circumstanced are to be carefully considered, and to the utmost provided for, it ought to be done as little as possible to the detriment of others, who may have greater leisure for purposes of daily devotion, and highly value the half hour,—nay, we may say, in the language of a well-known hymn—

> "the winged *hour*
> Spent in thy hallow'd courts, O Lord;"[1]

and who, especially in loneliness of life, in enfeebled health, or advancing age would thankfully linger somewhat longer, like Hannah of old, in the tabernacle at Shiloh,[2] in the rendering of thanks

---

[1] I need not, perhaps, more distinctly identify the hymn, familiar to the recollection of many, written by the late Rev. John William Cunningham, for more than fifty years vicar of Harrow-on-the-Hill; one of the parishes which were from old time peculiars of the See of Canterbury, and, as such, often visited, for confirmations or on like occasions, in former years, by Archbishop Howley.

> "Dear is the hallow'd morn to me,
>   When village bells awake the day;
> And, by their sacred minstrelsy,
>   Call me from earthly cares away.
> "And dear to me the winged hour
>   Spent in thy hallow'd courts, O Lord!
> To feel devotion's soothing power,
>   And catch the manna of thy word."

[2] 1 Sam. i. 12, "as she continued praying before the Lord," "Heb. *multiplied to pray*." Margin, A.V.

for past mercies, or for the alleviation of heavy
sorrows; in joining in His most worthy praise, in
hearing His most holy Word, or asking those
things which are requisite and necessary as well
for the body as the soul,[1] at the hands of Him, the
Holy One, who " inhabiteth the praises of Israel,"[2]
and hath left to his Church that most gracious
promise, for the support and comfort of her children, through all the days of their pilgrimage,
" Where *two or three* are gathered together in my
name, THERE AM I in the midst of them."[3] There
are, doubtless, those who seem to think brevity
the very essence of devotion, as it is confessedly
" the soul of wit," and also,—in the opinion,
apparently, of many persons,—the only, or, at
any rate, the highest excellence of a sermon.
There may be those to whom any prayers beyond
the very shortest are a weariness, or an effort to
which they are unequal, and which defeats its own
object. There may be—I do not presume to question it—those whose concentration of spirit may be
such as to enable them, within the smallest compass

---

[1] " And Hannah answered and said, . . . I am a woman of a sorrowful
spirit;" and "I . . . have poured out my soul before the Lord " (comp.
Ps. lxii. 8; cxlii. 1, 2); " for out of the abundance of my complaint (*or*,
' meditation ') and grief have I spoken hitherto." 1 Sam. i. 15, 16. Comp.
vv. 26, 27. " And she said, O my lord, as thy soul liveth, my lord, I
am the woman that stood by thee here, praying unto the LORD. For
this child I prayed; and the LORD hath given me my petition which I
asked of him."

[2] Ps. xxii. 3, " But thou art holy, O thou that inhabitest the praises
of Israel." (Bible Version.)

[3] S. Matt. xviii. 20.

of words, to realize varied wants, and the manifold
objects of comprehensive petitions; there may be
those who can bring, with sufficient vividness, before their mind's-eye the claims of their Queen and
country upon their devout and earnest thoughts, if
they hear only the brief versicle said, " O Lord,
save the Queen," with no repetition or reverting
to the theme ; or whose prayers for Christ's or-
dained servants, and for the whole body of His
Church, may, with the effectual fervency which
Christ's Apostle commends,[1] be summed up in that
other versicle, and the response to it, " Endue thy
ministers with righteousness. And make thy chosen
people joyful." But how many more they are—
we must, I think, admit—among the congregations
of worshippers in our churches, whose sense of
what is needed, and to be obtained by supplication
from on high, is deepened when we pray for all
the blessings on our Queen which our full daily
Office enumerates ; when again for " all the Royal
Family " we petition, " Endue them with thy holy
Spirit, enrich them with thy heavenly grace ; " or
when, yet again, " for the Clergy and people " we
put up such entreaties as these to Him " who
alone worketh great marvels "—supplications and
prayers which we, my Reverend Brethren, and
our faithful lay brethren alike, must feel we greatly
need, in the discharge of our difficult and weighty
office towards the flock of Christ, and to Him

---

[1] James v. 16.

whom in their persons we serve—"Send down
upon our Bishops, and Curates, and all Congregations committed to their charge, the healthful
Spirit of thy grace; and, that they may truly
please thee, pour upon them the continual dew of
thy blessing. Grant this, O Lord, for the honour
of our Advocate and Mediator, Jesus Christ." It
is important, I think, that it should be borne in
mind, that the Shortened Form for daily Service
was designed to meet a special want, not to super-
sede, or set aside, the Church's duly established
Order of Morning and Evening Prayer; and it may
not improperly be suggested, as a matter for consideration, whether, in towns where there are more
churches than one, and clergy and congregations
disposed to avail themselves of increased facilities
for assembling themselves thus together, arrangements might not be made by which, at one church,
there might be an early Service in the shortened
form, and in another, at a later hour, the ordinary
full Service. Above all, while we are anxious to
see the larger congregations in our churches, let us
not forget the privilege pledged to the "two or
three" by the sure promise of their Lord.

It has been further provided by the recent Act,
with a view to meet the case of town parishes, or
where there is a large population, "that an additional form of Service" may be used, varying
from any form prescribed by the Book of Common
Prayer; so that there be not introduced into such

additional Service any portion of the Order for the Administration of the Lord's Supper, or Holy Communion, or anything, except anthems or hymns, which does not form part of the Holy Scriptures or Book of Common Prayer; and so that such form of Service, and the mode in which it is used, is for the time being "approved by the Ordinary." It is obvious here that an opening is made for a great variety of ritual, with a very large exercise of private opinion and personal taste, limited only by the required consent of the Ordinary; and since this additional Service would very generally, I imagine, be the Service used by the evening congregation,—a Service commonly attended by large numbers,—there is occasion I think, for caution, in regard to the limits within which, and the conditions under which, the Clergy should avail themselves of this provision. The original appointment of the Ritual Commission, it may be well to bear in mind, arose out of varying interpretations put upon rules and orders which, meanwhile, had afforded much less scope for variety of practice: and the dissatisfaction thence arising in many quarters was thought urgently to demand inquiry, with a view "to secure general uniformity of practice in such matters as might be deemed essential." The result appears, somewhat singularly, to have been in the opposite direction, *viz.* that of a great increase· of freedom, and variety. Used discreetly and with moderation, such in-

creased liberty may, doubtless, be productive of
great benefit; but there is certainly need for care
and caution. There is in the present day, unques-
tionably, a great taste for novelty and variety; but
at the same time there is behind it, in the general
feeling of our people, and especially in those whose
feeling is entitled to the utmost consideration and
the most gentle treatment, a certain love of uniformity in sacred things, a desire to know what
they may expect to find when they go to church.
The principle of uniformity, moreover, is essentially
that of Catholicity. The strength of the Church, and
the joy of her members, in the early days of her un-
divided heritage, was that, wherever they went in
different lands, on whatever shores they were cast,
there were certain established forms of worship
everywhere to be found—" one Lord, one faith, one
baptism "[1]—liturgical forms, as our learned writers
on the Church's ritual, such as Bishop Beveridge,
Bishop Bull, and others have clearly shown, which
bore witness to a common origin in the earliest
days of the Apostolic Church.[2] And it was in
their desire to restore this unity in our own branch
of the Church Catholic that our truly Catholic-
minded Reformers, Cranmer and Ridley, going
back to the consent of earlier ages, when they
were compiling what they designed to make dis-

[1] Eph. iv. 5.
[2] See Bp. Bull's Sermon, "Common Prayers ancient, useful, and
necessary" (Sermon xiii.), Works, ed. Burton, vol. i., pp. 330-334.

tinctively " The Book of *Common* Prayer " for the
Church of England, provided, as we read in the Preface, that, " whereas heretofore there" had " been
great diversity in saying and singing within this
Realm; some following Salisbury use, some Hereford
use, and some the use of Bangor, some of York,
some of Lincoln, now from henceforth all the whole
Realm" should "have but one use." The unity which
they desired—and which, I think, we must feel
altogether they rightly desired—to secure would
easily be endangered by too free an exercise, even
by the general action of this or that Diocese, of the
liberty in question ; and as regards the individual
discretion of the clergyman in the formation of
new Services, we are significantly reminded, from
time to time, of the jealousy which would call for
stringent provisions, local or other, to restrict
possible vagaries of individual taste.[1] We do well
in endeavouring, within due limits, to make our
Services what is called " attractive " : but taste and
fashion are strangely variable and uncertain things,
and liable to constant reaction in one direction or
another.   And if we need to keep in mind, in
matters of public worship, the terms of our Blessed
Master's promise to the " two or three," we shall
also feel bound to remember the gracious favour
which He has declared towards *united* supplications:
" I say unto you," saith He, " if two or three shall
agree touching anything they shall ask on earth, it

---

[1] See Note A.

shall be done for them of my Father which is in heaven." We might easily, without due care, before we were altogether conscious of the change, lose the unity of the collective Church, in its Provincial and National constitution and action, and find ourselves unawares in something very like a " Congregational system."

There is yet another provision of the late Act which is open to some degree of ambiguity in its wording and application. " Upon any special occasion to be approved by the Ordinary, there may be used in any cathedral or church a special form of Service approved by the Ordinary, so that there be not introduced into such Service anything, except anthems or hymns, which does not form part of the Holy Scriptures or Book of Common Prayer." We have given us, in the Archbishop's Charge, his Grace's interpretation of this provision. " We have felt," said the Archbishop, " that *special occasions* arise in every parish, when it is desirable that there should be special prayers differing from the ordinary Service in use at the ordinary time. Such liberty of introducing special Services *for harvest festivals, or on an occasion of any great sudden judgment which happens to visit a neighbourhood, or for any other remarkable occasion,* is now sanctioned by the authorities of the Church and State." This is, certainly, what would suggest itself, to anyone, as the obvious meaning of the provision in question ; and so the Archbishop under-

stands it. But there appears to be a disposition in
some quarters, on the strength of this enactment,
to provide new "special" Services for solemn days
or seasons in our sacred year, for which the Church
would seem to have already made what she regarded as suitable provision in her regularly
appointed order.[1]

In immediate connection with this point, I would
notice a provision in the Act of the preceding
year, the "Prayer Book (Tables of Lessons) Act,"
which appears to be open, in a still greater degree,
to doubt, and liability to confusion. It is provided
"that *upon occasions to be appointed by the Ordinary*, other Psalms may, with his consent, be substituted for those appointed in the Psalter." This
provision formed no part of the Report of the
Ritual Commission which came before Convocation;
nor was it approved by Convocation in any such
extensive form. The words found in the Act,
"upon occasions to be *appointed* by the Ordinary,"
originated, there is no doubt, in a clerical error, or
misprint, of the word "appointed" for "approved":
as is evident, indeed, from the context, which runs
thus—"upon occasions to be *approved* by the Ordinary, other Psalms may, *with his consent*, be substituted for those appointed in the Psalter." The
provision was, in fact, in its original intention,
when proposed in the Ritual Commission, strictly
parallel with that other contained in the Act,

[1] See Note B.

"that upon occasions to be *approved* by the Ordinary, other *Lessons* may, with his consent, be substituted for those which are appointed in the Calendar." The minister, to whose discretion it was left, would apply for the *approval* and *consent* of the Ordinary. On the strength, however, of this provision, in one large and important Diocese, followed herein, I believe, by another neighbouring Diocese, a Table of special Psalms has been appointed by the Ordinary,—exercising the authority regarded as thus given to him (though indeed, the word "approved" appears in the ordinance of the Diocesan),—not simply for the few marked days specified in the Lower House of Convocation when the subject was dealt with there, *viz.* Advent Sunday, the Circumcision, the Epiphany, the Annunciation, Easter Eve, and Trinity Sunday, but also for the Thursday before Easter, Michaelmas Day, all days of Apostles, and other Festivals.[1] In the last case in particular, it is provided, in the Diocesan ordinance in question, that "when the Psalms in the Daily Order are less appropriate, any of" some thirteen which are specified, "may be used, at the discretion of the Minister." It is an extensive superseding of the appointed order of the Prayer Book, for which a precedent would thus be set; and it becomes the more serious, when it is remembered that there is a previous provision of the Prayer Book, that, "whensoever Proper Psalms or Lessons

[1] See Note C.

are appointed, then the Psalms and Lessons of
ordinary course appointed in the Psalter and
Calendar (if they be different) shall be omitted
for that time." The Church, in the Preface to her
Book of Common Prayer, has so clearly defined,
—and so greatly to the advantage of us all,—
the relations of Minister, Bishop, and people,
guarding the rights of each, that I cannot but
commend it to your practical consideration, my
Reverend Brethren, whether it be not our wisdom
to be somewhat sparing in our recourse to enactments which appear open to grave question and
doubt as to their correct application; and which
may imperil, unless due care be exercised, the
rights and privileges which they seem to extend,
but which they may in practice seriously compro-
mise; endangering meanwhile the harmony which
the Church would desire to secure.

One other point I should wish to notice in the
provisions of the recent Act. "It was felt," to
avail myself again of the Archbishop's words,
"that there might be in many of our parishes,
especially in towns, difficulties from the length of
the Services, . . . and hence it was distinctly sanctioned by the legislation of last session, that, in
cases where it was found desirable, Services might
be divided. Many held," said his Grace, "that
this could lawfully be done before; but doubts
existed; and it was thought best to have a distinct
assertion of the legislative authority both of the

Church and State, that there was nothing irre-
gular, or belonging to any particular sect or party,
in this dividing of the Services." When this
matter was before Convocation, I confess to having
felt some anxiety, lest what might look like a direct
Parliamentary interpretation, of rubrics supposed
to be doubtful, should interfere with the duty
and right of interpretation in such cases recog-
nized, in the Preface to the Prayer Book, as vested
in the Bishops of the Church. I thought it right,
therefore, to bring this point, by a distinct repre-
sentation, since attention had not been called to it,
under the consideration of his Grace the President
and their Lordships of the Upper House. His Grace
was pleased to express his opinion of its importance; and I was glad to find that the clause in
the Act, which dealt with this matter, was worded
thus—that "whereas doubts have arisen as to
whether the following forms of Service, that is to
say, the Order for Morning Prayer, the Litany,
and the Order for the Administration of the Lord's
Supper, or Holy Communion, may be used as separate Services, and it is expedient to remove such
doubts; be it therefore enacted and declared, that
any such forms of Service may be used together, or
in varying order as separate Services . . . . *without
prejudice, nevertheless, to any legal powers vested in
the Ordinary.*" The interpretation itself thus sanctioned in regard to division of the Services was, in
fact, that which, I believe, had been generally re-

cognized and acted upon by the Bishops; although if there was any opening for a legal doubt in the interpretation of the Act of Uniformity, it was proper that in the "Act of Uniformity Amendment Act" such opening for doubt should be closed.

In reference to the separate use of the Services in question, I think it well to point out that, while it is thus made clear that these Services may be used separately, there is no authority given to use them otherwise than in their integrity. I speak with reference particularly to " the Order for the Administration of the Lord's Supper, or Holy Communion." It is a Service bearing the marks upon it of so much careful consideration of the several component parts of what the Office itself describes as " those holy mysteries," compiled as it was in the midst of serious divisions in Christendom, and " deep thoughts of heart," that we should run great risk, assuredly, in taking part of it, as an appendage to other Services, and omitting the rest. The earlier part of the Service, in particular, oc- cupies a very important place in connection with what follows. The Collect for Purity, the rehears- ing of the Ten Commandments, with the responsive petitions for pardon and grace, the solemn repeti- tion of the Creed, these form the fitting approach to sacred rites requiring special self-examina- tion, deep repentance, and a true faith, in them that approach; and the Exhortation which precedes the Confession, and which there seems a prevailing disposition to omit, has, perhaps, a special fitness, and not the reverse, in connection with more frequent Communion; reminding us, as it does, " how St. Paul exhorteth *all* persons diligently to try and examine themselves," before they approach that holy Table; and, moreover, containing the fullest enumeration given in the Service of the privileges and blessings of that high Communion,[1] as well as of the danger, of which the Apostle had warned his converts, of "not discerning the Lord's body."[2] Bishop Ridley, in his last Farewell, " written a little before he suffered," spoke feelingly, in allusion to the then suppressed Book of Common Prayer, of what " this Church of England had of late, of the infinite goodness and abundant grace of Almighty God; great substance, great riches of heavenly treasure, great plenty of God's true and sincere word, the true and wholesome administration of Christ's Sacraments, the whole profession of Christ's religion truly and plainly set forth in Baptism." " This Church had also," he said, "a true and sincere form and manner of the Lord's Supper."[3] And it may be of no small importance, that that whole " form and manner" of Celebration and Communion should be carefully observed and maintained in its

---

[1] " For as the benefit is great, if with a true penitent heart and lively faith we receive that holy Sacrament; (for then we spiritually eat the flesh of Christ, and drink his blood; then we dwell in Christ, and Christ in us; we are one with Christ, and Christ with us;")—

[2] Compare 1 Cor. xi. 27–30.

[3] Life of Bp. Ridley, by Dr. Gloucester Ridley.

full integrity, "according to the proportion of faith."
The Order of the Prayer Book, duly followed as it
stands, is a witness and preservative, on the one
hand, against Roman corruption of primitive
doctrine and ritual, and on the other hand against
the low Zuinglian, or Socinian, view which would
willingly recognize a feast of love, a Christian
agape, a token of brotherly unity, while it would
gladly omit the confession of faith and hope in
Him, our Saviour, Christ, both God and Man, "the
Only Begotten Son of God, Begotten of his Father
before all worlds, God of God, Light of Light, Very
God of Very God, Begotten not made, of One substance with the Father," "in whom" alone "we have
redemption through His blood, even the Remission
of sins,"[1] and "look for the Resurrection of the
dead, and the life of the world to come."

You will not be of opinion, I think, my Reverend
Brethren, that I have occupied your time unduly
by entering thus fully into the legislative provisions
which have been made since we last met in Visitation, and to which his Grace the Archbishop
directed your particular attention last year.[2] It
will seem to you, I am persuaded, of some importance that it should be perfectly understood what,
precisely, those provisions are, and that they should
be guarded from any misapprehension abroad in
regard to them. The Archbishop characterized

[1] Eph. i. 7; Col. i. 14.   [2] See Note D.

the changes which had thus been made, as "the greatest which have been introduced in such a matter since the time of Charles II."; and observed that, "of course, if we have made some which prove to be beneficial, we shall naturally consider whether there are any still before us." "I believe we shall find," said his Grace, "that the mode in which alone such changes can legitimately be introduced is a safeguard against any rash innovation." That only mode, I need hardly say, to which the Archbishop referred, as that by which such changes could be introduced, is by the regular and constitutional action of Convocation preparatory to any measures in Parliament. We shall hear no more, I trust, in popular talk, of "a short Bill" to be brought in at once, without the consent of Convocation, to settle this matter or that.

Of other matters which were dealt with by the Ritual Commission, and which have since been brought under the consideration of Convocation, I have the less occasion to speak, because they are, some of them, still in process of examination and discussion. On one of these subjects—a matter of great importance, and one which has deeply stirred the mind of the Church, as touching one of her ancient Creeds—the Lower House of Convocation, to which the subject was specially referred by the Upper House, has, after full, and patient, and careful consideration, pronounced very decisively its judgment. A very large Com-

mittee of both Houses, including the whole of the
Upper House, and, according to custom and privilege, twice that number of the Lower, has also
presented its Report, which has since been considered by the Lower House, and now remains to
be dealt with by the Upper House, if to their
Lordships it shall so seem fit.[1]

Upon matters which have come before Parliament, or which are at the present time awaiting
its decision, I will not detain you now; because,
inasmuch as they are of a mixed nature, of a temporal as well as partly of a spiritual character, we
may, I hope, have an opportunity for some conference, in regard to them, of the Clergy and Laity
present to-day, after the business of the Visitation
Court is gone through.

In regard only to the Burials Bill which is now
before the House of Commons, having passed the
Second Reading, and now awaiting the going into
Committee—which will be opposed—I would just
observe, that it presents the most extraordinary
instance that ever was witnessed, I suppose, in a
like matter, of a sudden and complete " change of
front," if I may so describe it, of the forces con-
federated against us.   In the days of Church-rate
controversy, we were wont to remind the opponents
of Church-rates that if, as they pleaded, they did
not use our Churches, and had their own places of
worship to support, they had at least an interest in

---

[1] See Note E.

our Churchyards; to say nothing of the use they often made of the Church itself for marriage rites; and that if they desired, as so many of them did, to be laid beside their fathers in the old Church-yard, they might well be willing to contribute something to the repair of the Churchyard wall, or of the bell which was to toll at their burial. But no, they would none of it : and men, wearied out at last, granted them their petition; and the care and cost of the Churchyard was, by the abolition of all compulsory enforcement, thrown upon Churchmen, as what, it was said, belonged properly to them, and to them alone, to pay. And now, all this notwithstanding, the Churchyard is claimed as " national property" for all sects and de-nominations, for people of all religions or none, to use as of equal right and proprietorship undoubted.

If it were only a little pardonable inconsistency, or shortness of memory, in simple-minded men with which we had to deal, or if it were only a slight personal favour or indulgence that were concerned, we might well, my Reverend Brethren, be willing on our own part, and our lay brethren with us, to be somewhat forgetful. But they with whom we are concerned do not allow us for a moment to be unmindful, that it is a great principle for which they are contending: and, by consequence, so are we. We were told by them long ago—some twenty years since—that, in the parishes in Essex mainly concerned, " the interest of the Church-rate struggle was gone comparatively into insignificance *per se*, and was considered as a matter of great interest only as bearing upon the really important question, in their estimation, of the separation of Church and State." And they believed that they had " in these Church-rate battles the very best vantage ground for advancing that question, which of all others, was, in their estimation, *the question of the age.*" [1]

It is the same question now, under a new phase, and with new tactics of warfare. It is no question, —let it be well borne in mind—no question, as it was in a former age, as to what form of religion or Church polity—as, for instance, Episcopacy or Presbyterianism —was most in accordance with Scripture, and best entitled to national preference; no question of personal freedom to worship God according to the dictates of individual conscience, no man forbidding or hindering; it is no question of State patronage or State endowment, to be bestowed equally, or proportionably, upon all: there is now an open repudiation of anything like what is designated as "concurrent endowment"; it is simple "SECULARIZATION" that is in view.[2] The principle runs throughout, in Education and Religion alike. In regard to Education, in former years we were told that, "according to the conscientious convictions of the religious bodies

---

[1] See Evidence given before a Select Committee of the House of Commons on Church-rates, 1853; largely quoted in a Charge delivered in 1854. [2] See Note F.

of this country, the school" was a "part of the
machinery of a Christian congregation," and that
"education was primarily a religious institution."[1]
But now it is to be transferred bodily to the State;
and the State, it is laid down, can have no religion;
and Education is therefore to be secularized. And
as it fares with the village school, on such principles as these, so it fares also with the Church
and the Churchyard. The land which, in Anglo-
Saxon times, the lords of the soil gave for God's
house and "God's acre,"—as the plot of ground
which was given for the resting place of His
saints and servants was religiously named,—is, by
a strange anachronism and historic falsehood, pronounced to be "national property," knowing nothing of a Redeemer that liveth, and shall stand at
our latter day upon the earth, or of a Resurrection
of the dead through Him. Meanwhile, all that
gives its value to the village churchyard, and that
might well make men wish to be laid there—its
sacredness,—would, in the very nature of things, be
gone; "the *sacred* calm that breathes around," in
the expressive words of the well-known "Elegy,"
as it came originally from the poet's pen—

"In still small accents whispering from the ground,
A grateful earnest of eternal peace"—

all this would be gone for ever.

I believe, my Reverend Brethren, whether as

[1] See the semi-official volume, put forth in 1847, 'The Church,
the School, and the Congregation.'

regards Education or Worship, our Churches or
our Schools, if we be but true to ourselves, to the
principles of our Church, as embodied in our
Prayer Book, and to our infallible Guide, the Word
of God, taking it as "a lantern to our feet, and a
light to our path," amidst whatever difficulties and
perplexities of the varying hour that path may lie;
watching the signs of the times, and the varied
perils which surround us, we have nothing to fear
from the designs of our enemies. The feeling
which has shown itself far and wide among our
people, in resolute attachment to the principle of
religious education, and earnest deprecation of any
interference with it, is one more proof, in confirmation of others which have been vouchsafed to us of
late, that there are, beneath the surface of that portion of the vineyard which hath been given to us
to cultivate, springs of thought and feeling which
need but the occasion to call them forth to show
their influence and power. There are signs everywhere around us, in regard to the so-called "disestablishment and disendowment" of the Church,
or in other words—for it is nothing less than this—
the dethroning Christ our Lord from His Sove-
reignty as "the Prince of the kings of the earth,"
and robbing Him of the gifts which His servants
in past days, in the spirit of lowly homage to HIM,
and pious care for His poor, have devoted to Him,
and laid upon His altar,—that men are rising up
to a true sense of the momentous issues at stake,

and prepared to resist, in good earnest, Sacrilege
and Desecration, Robbery and Wrong.

"Then draw we nearer," let me say, in conclusion, in the words of the revered poet of our
'Christian Year'—

> " Then draw we nearer day by day,
>   Each to his brethren, all to God ;
>   Let the world take us as she may,
>   We must not change our road."[1]

Avoiding with charitable care everything—in our
teaching or action ; in our public ministrations,
or in our daily walk and conversation among our
brethren,—everything which might cause needless
division, arouse prejudice, even though it were un-
reasonable, or create mistrust, however unfounded ;
" giving no offence in anything, that the ministry
be not blamed," let us seek to be found " in all
things approving ourselves as the ministers of God,
in much patience, in afflictions," if need be, and
oftentimes "in necessities, in distresses," but always,
assuredly, " in labours, in watchings, in fastings ;
by pureness, by knowledge, by kindness, by long-
suffering, by the Holy Ghost, by love unfeigned,
by the word of truth, by the power of God, by the
armour of righteousness on the right hand and on
the left, by honour and dishonour, by evil report
and good report : as deceivers, and yet true ; as
dying, and, behold, we live ; as chastened, and not
killed ; as sorrowful, yet alway rejoicing ; as poor,

----

[1] THE CHRISTIAN YEAR ; Second Sunday after Trinity.

yet making many rich; as having nothing, and yet possessing all things."[1]

Even so, by our various ministries, in our several offices and functions, as "many members" of "one body in Christ, and every one members of one another;"[2] "as every man hath received the gift, even so ministering the same one to another, as good stewards of the manifold grace of God;"[3] even thus, by our humble duty and service rendered as unto Christ, unto Him that is able to do exceeding abundantly above all that we ask or think, according to the power that worketh in us, unto him be glory in the Church by Christ Jesus throughout all ages, world without end. Amen."[4]

[1] 2 Cor. iv. 3–10.   [2] Rom. xii. 4, 5.   [3] 1 Pet. iv. 10.
[4] Eph. iii. 20, 21.

NOTE A.

It may not be uninstructive to recall to mind the popular impressions conveyed, when the budget of Liturgical reform in contemplation was opened, at the end of 1871, as grounded on the last Report of the Rubrical Commission. It was described, with something of exaggeration, not perhaps altogether extraordinary, as taking " the opinion of Convocation whether it would not be well to get rid of uniformity as far as possible ;" and the proposal, it was truly enough observed, was "the singular result of the Commission appointed four years" before " to consider how to promote greater uniformity 'in such matters as may be deemed essential.'" "The Law Courts," it was said, had " taken out of the hands of the Ritual Commissioners those points of dress and ceremonial which they were more especially appointed to consider." Of the new " Lectionary," which was grounded on the Commissioners' Third Report, it was observed, that " one of its leading characteristics was that it was far more elastic than the old Table ; and as both would be lawful for some nearly ten years longer, the public" would " probably have some opportunity for estimating the advantage of diversity, and of appreciating 'the discretion of the minister.'" In their Fourth Report, however, it was alleged, " the Commissioners ventured on a general series of recommendations which went much/further in relaxing the ancient rigidity of the Church of England." It appeared (so it was said) as if the Church was " suddenly invited to change front, and to ask Parliament to vest in the Clergy and the Bishops an indefinite discretion in the arrangement of the Services." For, besides the freedom sanctioned in regard to the order of the Services, it was now proposed that, " in a third Service on Sundays, the minister should be at liberty, with the approval of the Ordinary, to use any other form of Service whatsoever, so that the words be selected from the Prayer Book ;" and it was " similarly proposed that on week days, instead of the regular daily prayers, any form of Service taken from the Prayer Book and similarly approved, should be lawful. It would be interesting," said the writer of this review of the various proposals concerned, " to calculate the permutations and combinations possible among some scores of prayers." It

was further " proposed, that when the Queen" had " been prayed
for in a preceding Service, the prayer for the Queen in the Communion Service " might be omitted ; " the time of the Service at
which the Sermon is to be preached" might " be varied ; the
Communion Office " might " be modified by more than one omission, including that of the Ten Commandments, at the discretion
of the minister, subject to the discretion of the Ordinary. Not
to dwell on similar minor alterations, a most material elasticity "
was " to be introduced into the Burial Service, and the standing
dispute respecting the peril of the unbaptized or excommuni-
cated " was " evaded by leaving it to the discretion of the clergyman to read a few short sentences from Scripture, together with
the Lord's Prayer."

" It will take away the breath of many excellent people," said
the writer, " to hear that these sweeping changes are actually to
be proposed, ... and that they may find themselves before
many months unable to tell, on entering a strange church, what
part of the Prayer Book they will hear read, and not even sure
whether they will again hear the famous Lesson which has
fallen, for so many generations, on the ears of English mourners."
Amidst whatever feelings of satisfaction were expressed in regard to " a list of relaxations," many of which offered " a relief
which the majority of Churchmen had desired for years," it was
plainly said, " When we come to consider whether the simple
method proposed by the Commissioners will be likely to commend itself as the solution of the problem, it is impossible not
to discover a difficulty which has already attracted attention in
Parliament." " Under the existing law," namely, " a layman
at least knows what he may expect, and can claim the due per-
formance of known Offices. He may wish these Offices modified
and varied : but will he be content that the Clergy should do it
at their own pleasure ? In short, is not some such proposal as
that of Lord Sandon for Parochial Councils an inevitable
supplement of such a general relaxation of uniform rule as this
proposal involves ? " ('Times,' Dec. 28, 1871.)

Happily, Convocation modified essentially some of these
proposals before they were carried into a law. And in regard to
the first point noticed in the preceding Charge, it may be observed, Convocation did what in it lay distinctly to mark that
the shortened order of daily Service was not intended to be a
substitute for the regular form of Morning and Evening Prayer,

but simply as allowing certain *omissions* to be made, if need be,
in those forms. And further, after as careful a consideration
in detail as was possible, it has defined—and the definition has
been embodied in the Uniformity Act Amendment Act—*what*
omissions may be there allowed; so as to have the consentient
judgment of the Convocations of the two Provinces to determine
the matter, and not the discretion of each individual minister
with the approval simply of his Ordinary. Then, again, in
regard to matters more recently discussed in the Lower House
of Convocation, the omissions, proposed by the Ritual Commissioners, of the Collect for the Queen, the recital of the Commandments, &c., were rejected by the House; as also the various
alternative Lessons proposed in the Burial Service. A " third
Service" for Sundays has also been prepared by a Committee of
the Lower House, which would secure something like uniformity, and protect the congregations of our people from endless
variations in the forms of Service proposed.

NOTE B.

The reference here made was, in particular, to the solemn
season of Holy Week, and Good Friday, above all. The Church
of England has appointed what she deemed fitting and appropriate services for the sacred day of Christ's Passion; and anyone going into a Church of England church on Good Friday
would naturally expect to find the service appointed in the
Prayer Book going on—not " Tenebræ," or the like—and would
be justified in such an expectation. But every kind of " will-
worship" for Good Friday might be introduced as a " Special
Service;" however little in harmony with the mind and feeling
of the Church.

This year there appeared in the papers a notice :—

" At three o'clock to-morrow (Good Friday) afternoon, there
will be a *special service* in the nave of Westminster Abbey,
with a sermon by the Dean. A *shortened form* of evening
prayer will be sung as far as the third Collect, Psalm 88 being
sung to a chant, by Flintoft, and the ' Nunc Dimittis ' to Elvey
in A. The sermon will then be preached, and on its conclusion
what are commonly known as the ' Passion ' numbers in the
' Messiah ' will be sung as an anthem. Tickets for this service
are to be obtained on application to the Dean."

It does not exactly appear how this "Special Service" was authorized by the recent Act. Good Friday is one of the days on which the "shortened form" is not allowed to be used, in place of the Order for Evening Prayer; and it does not appear that the regular Evening Prayer was said at another hour on that day, in the Abbey.

The same paper from which the above is extracted had just given a notice, in reference to a church in the neighbourhood of London, "Handel's Passion Music is to be sung this evening by the members of the London Church Choir Association. The service will commence at half-past seven." Then followed a notice that "a selection from Bach's Passion Music" was "to be introduced as *a special service*" that night, at one of our cathedrals.

Whenever it is desired now-a-days to gather a large congregation, it seems to be thought necessary to advertize a "Special Service." Sometimes the services themselves do not turn out to be so "special" as they might appear. On the 8th of May last there appeared an announcement, as follows :—

"A special service in connection with the Church of England Sunday School Institute is to be held this evening at St. Paul's Cathedral at seven o'clock. The choir will consist of a large body of the members of the London Diocesan Lay Helpers' Association, assisted by the choir of All Saints', Margaret Street; Mr. W. Stevenson Hoyte, the organist and choirmaster of that church, *conducting the entire service from the lectern.* Mr. Hoyte will also play the opening and concluding voluntaries upon the organ, including an Andante in G, by Smart, Fantaisie in F minor, by Mozart, and a Toccata and Fugue, by J. S. Bach. The Rev. Daniel Moore, Chaplain in Ordinary to the Queen, will preach the sermon."

On inquiry being made of the authorities of St. Paul's as to the nature of this "Special Service," it appeared that it was simply the Evening Prayer, with these musical appendages.

A "special service in Canterbury Cathedral" was lately announced in a notice put forth in behalf of a Diocesan Society; but when it was inquired at the Cathedral what was the "specialty" in the service, it was found that the service was appointed to be "at eleven o'clock," instead of at ten, or half-past ten, the accustomed hour.

NOTE C.

This provision, in regard to the appointment or approval of Psalms for special occasions, formed no part of the Bill as originally brought into the House of Lords, nor in the Bill as brought from the Lords and printed for the House of Commons. It appears to have found its way into the Bill, without discussion and notice of any sort, as it passed through Committee of the House of Commons.

Nor, as is stated in the Charge, did it form any part of the [Third] Report of the Ritual Committee, which is referred to in the Bill as the original basis of legislation; nor was it approved by Convocation in any such extensive form as it appears to take in the Act.

The facts of the case, which it is of some importance that Churchmen should rightly understand, are briefly these.

In the Session of Feb. 9, 1870, on the motion of the Bishop of Winchester, seconded by the Bishop of Llandaff, the Bishop of London presiding in the absence of the Archbishop, an Address was adopted as follows:—

" We humbly pray your Majesty to be graciously pleased to direct, that there be laid before the Convocation of the Province of Canterbury the Report of a Royal Commission which your Majesty was pleased to issue on certain proposed alterations in the Calendar, with the Table of Lessons appointed in the Book of Common Prayer for public reading in our churches."

In moving this resolution, the Bishop of Winchester said:— " I need not say to any of your Lordships, that the regular form for making any sort of alteration in that most sacred depository of the Church, the Book of Common Prayer, is that the Convocations of the two Provinces should be consulted, and should give to her Majesty their judgment upon it. Of course it cannot take effect legally until Parliament, with her Majesty at the head, has also pronounced upon it. This has been the universal course hitherto adopted; and as I doubt not that your Lordships are most anxious that such a course should continue, and as I am persuaded of her Majesty's gracious readiness to bring the matter before us, I trust there will be no opposition to the motion,—that this Address, with the consent of the Lower House, be presented to her Majesty." ('Chron. of Convocation,' 1870, pp. 2, 3.)

The consent and concurrence of the Lower House, on the motion of the Dean of Canterbury, seconded by the Dean of Westminster, was, on the same day, unanimously given. (Ibid., p. 40.)

It is not necessary here to enter on any further particulars in regard to this Address, or the answer returned to it; or as to the Joint Committee appointed to consider the Report of the Commission, or any proceedings of either House in reference to the Report of the Joint Committee, or connected with it. We will confine our attention simply to the question respecting special *Psalms*. In the Session of May 3 (1870) the Bishop of Lincoln, in the Upper House, said, it appears, that there was one question, in connection with the matter which the House had just dealt with, which he "should like to refer to, as in the nature of a *casus omissus* in the Lectionary." He thought it was "desirable that some arrangement should be made with regard to having Proper Psalms on particular days;" and he went on to specify Trinity Sunday, Easter Eve, and 'the Epiphany, as days on which the want was felt. "I have had a communication," said his Lordship, "with one of the ablest ritualists of our day, who possesses a most excellent ritual library, I mean the present Dean of Trinity College, Cambridge, Mr. H. J. Hotham. He has made good use of his valuable library, and he has communicated to me the result of his researches as to the Proper Psalms used in the ancient rites, specially in Sarum, that being distinctly Anglican. I should suppose that it would be very desirable that we should place ourselves in relation with the ancient Church of Sarum, not merely as to the Lessons of Scripture, but as to the selection of the Psalms on great festive occasions and other solemnities of the Church. I do not know whether it would be quite in order to propose this as a resolution. I would rather raise it as a question; but this is the sort of motion that I would, if necessary, submit :—

"' That an addition be made to the " Table of Proper Psalms on certain days," and that Proper Psalms be appointed for the following Holy Days—*viz.* the Feast of Circumcision, or New Year's Day; the Feast of Epiphany, or the Manifestation of Christ to the Gentiles; the Feast of the Annunciation; Thursday before Easter, Easter Eve, Trinity Sunday. Also that Proper Psalms be appointed for Church Dedications and Harvest Festivals; and that in the selection of those Psalms special attention be paid to the Psalms appointed respectively for these occasions in the ancient use of the Church of Sarum.'

" This is the question I wish to bring before the House. As to the manner of dealing with it, I would rather be instructed on that by others."

The question was asked, " Could not the Ritual Commissioners propose it ? " The Bishop of Lincoln replied, " I have proposed it to them. They wished to do it, but they thought that their powers did not extend so far. I have already sounded several members of the Ritual Commission. I do not know that they might not do it, but they did not seem to think that they could."

The question, it was agreed, should be postponed to a future occasion. "In the meantime," said his Lordship, "I suppose I am at liberty to communicate it to the Ritual Commission."

The Bishop accordingly, a few days after (May 6), addressed a letter to the Ritual Commission, which is to be found in the Appendix to the Fourth Report, p. 160.

At the meeting of the Ritual Commission (the 105th), held May 19, the letter was taken into consideration. " The Bishop of Gloucester and Bristol moved, and Mr. Buxton seconded,

" ' That the Commission desires to record its best thanks to the Bishop of Lincoln for his communication touching the Proper Psalms, and, having ascertained that his proposals are in their judgment sufficiently provided for by a general Rubric, which has been ·drawn up by the Commission, do not feel it desirable to make the Special Table of Psalms as suggested by him.'

" To which Mr. Humphry moved as an amendment, which was seconded by Canon Gregory,

" ' That the Bishop of Lincoln's suggestions be referred to a Special Committee.'

" A division was first taken upon the amendment, when 8 votes were given for it, and 12 against it.

" A division was then taken upon the original motion, when 9 votes were given for, and 2 against it." (Fourth Report, p. 125.)

The " general Rubric " referred to in this resolution, as already passed, and appearing to the Commissioners to answer the purpose, was as follows, and had been thus brought about.

At the (68th) meeting, held April 16, 1869, "The order how the Psalter is appointed to be read" having been read by the Secretary,

" The Bishop of Oxford moved, and Earl Beauchamp seconded:

" ' Upon special occasions to be approved by the Ordinary, Proper Psalms may, with his consent, be substituted for those which are appointed in the Psalter.'

" Upon a division the motion was agreed to, *nemine contradicente.*

" Canon Payne Smith then moved, and Mr. Humphry seconded :

" ' That a Committee be appointed to select Psalms for alternative use on Sundays, and for such Holy Days as may seem to require it.'

" Upon a division, 4 votes were given for, and 9 against, the motion."

It was consequently lost. However, at the meeting (74th), held on June 3, 1869,

" Upon the order how the Psalter is appointed to be read being read by the Secretary, Lord Ebury moved that the consideration of it be adjourned for a week, in order to enable him to prepare and circulate a paper upon it.

" Upon a division, 9 votes were given for, and 4 against, the motion, and the subject was accordingly adjourned." (Report, p. 99.)

Three weeks afterwards (78th meeting), June 24, 1869, we find,

" Upon the motion of the Dean of Ely, the Minute adopted on April 16, with reference to Proper Psalms to be substituted on special occasions, was read by the Secretary ; and it was agreed that upon a revision such Minute should be considered as open to amendment." (Report, p. 101.)

Accordingly at the (88th) meeting, held February 1, 1870,

" The following new Rubric, provisionally adopted on April 16, 1869, was then read by the Secretary :—

" ' Upon special occasions, to be approved by the Ordinary, Proper Psalms may, with his consent, be substituted for those which are appointed in the Psalter.'

" The Bishop of Carlisle moved, and the Dean of Westminster seconded, that the new Rubric be amended as follows :—

" ' Upon occasions, to be approved by the Ordinary, other

Psalms may, with his consent, be substituted for those which are appointed in the Psalter.'

"Mr. Perry also moved, and Mr. Humphry seconded, that the Rubric be amended as follows :—

"'Upon occasions, approved by the Ordinary, other Psalms may be substituted for those appointed to be read daily.'

"A division was first taken upon the Bishop of Carlisle's motion, when 10 votes were given for, and 4 against it, and Mr. Perry's motion was therefore not put.

"Mr. Humphry then moved, that in the Rubric, as now amended, the words 'with his consent' be omitted; but upon a division 5 votes were given for, and 12 against it." (Report, p. 109.)

Meanwhile, at the (87th) meeting, held January 12, 1870, when the Third Report had been under consideration for final adoption :

"The Dean of Westminster then moved, and Mr. Humphry seconded, to add after paragraph eight the following words :—

"'We recommend that, upon occasions to be approved by the Ordinary, Proper Psalms may, with his consent, be substituted for those which are appointed in the Psalter.'

"But after discussion, the motion was, by leave, withdrawn." (Report, p. 109.) This Rubric, therefore, was deliberately not included among the recommendations of the *Third* Report.

At the first meeting, therefore, of the Upper House, in the group of Sessions of Convocation held later in the season, July 5 (1870), in the absence of the Bishop of Lincoln, the Bishop of Winchester said, "I am very earnestly requested by the Bishop of Lincoln to propose a resolution to carry out one of the recommendations of the Ritual Commission, and have great pleasure in doing so: 'That an humble address be presented to her Majesty, praying her Majesty to direct the necessary steps to be taken to empower the Bishop of any diocese to allow of the use of Special Psalms on special occasions; and that this resolution be communicated to the Lower House.'" The motion was seconded by the Bishop of Hereford and agreed to.

On the day following, in the Lower House, the Prolocutor interrupted the discussion which was going on on the subject of

Cathedral Chapters, to communicate this and another resolution of the Upper House, and read the address proposed. The Prolocutor added, " I have in reference to these matters to say that I have received a letter from the presiding Bishop, in which he says he has no wish to interfere with the usual course of business of this House; but that it is most desirable that the address to the Queen should be taken into consideration as soon as possible." ('Chronicle of Convocation,' p. 479.)

The next day, accordingly, in the course of the discussion on the same subject, the Prolocutor said that, before calling upon the next speaker, he wished to communicate to the House, that their Lordships of the Upper House were " desirous that the Address which was sent down for approval" the day before, " with regard to the appointment of Proper Psalms for special occasions, should be returned to the Upper House as soon as possible. Perhaps," said the Prolocutor, " if the resolution does not require discussion, the House will allow me to put it. I may mention that this is a matter in which one of the most honoured members of Convocation, Dr. Wordsworth, now Bishop of Lincoln, takes great interest. The object of the proposal is that there should be Proper Psalms appointed to certain Festivals."

The adoption of the resolution by the Upper House having been moved and seconded, the Dean of Canterbury observed, in reference to Cathedrals, that hitherto it had " been the duty of the Dean to appoint Proper Psalms when they seem to be required," but it now appeared that they were to apply to the Bishop of the diocese to appoint Psalms. He therefore asked, " Should we not substitute the word ' Ordinary' for ' Bishop' ; " and the Prolocutor offered " to suggest that alteration to their Lordships." Thereupon Canon Jebb, " with a perfect recognition of the ancient right of the Bishops to appoint special services for special occasions," thought that this was " a period at which the House should regard with the utmost jealousy any attempt to alter the Prayer Book. It is all very well," said Dr. Jebb, " for the Bishops, on their own authority, to appoint Lessons or Psalms for special occasions ; but to alter the Psalms on the great Festivals, desirable as it might be in itself, would be a most essential alteration of the Prayer Book ; and I do not think it ought to be undertaken unless with the sanction and supervision of Convocation itself."

" The Prolocutor.—I have been requested by the Bishop of Lincoln, who takes special interest in this subject, to state that the object of the Address to her Majesty is to obtain power to appoint Psalms for Ascension Day,* Trinity Sunday, and the Epiphany; and for such special occasions as Harvest Services; and for a third service on Sunday.

" Canon Jebb.—Then the discretion of the Bishops is to be limited to that extent ?

" The Prolocutor.—I believe it to be so.

" Archdeacon Clark.—What the Upper House recommended is, that we should ask the Queen to authorize the Bishops to appoint Special Psalms for special occasions, not, as I understand, the great Festivals of the Church, but Harvest Services, and occasions of that kind ; but the Bishop of Lincoln seems to contemplate something more than that; and the House should be quite clear on that point before we vote.

" Canon Riddell.—I think that, connecting what is now proposed with the letter of the Bishop of Lincoln, it is impossible to doubt that the power in question is intended to apply to the Epiphany and other Festivals of the Church for which no special Psalms are appointed. The House must not overlook the Bill which has been introduced into the House of Lords by the Lord Chancellor It appears to me as if we are now virtually about to ask Parliament, in addition to sanctioning a new Lectionary, to give new and important powers to the Bishops.

" Prebendary Fagan.—I move the addition of the following words :—' That, in reference to the great stated Festivals of the Church, this House earnestly prays that there may be one general agreement on the part of the Bishops as to the Psalms to be selected.'

" Canon Selwyn.—May I ask what you think is the meaning of the word ' empower,' as used in the words, ' to ask her Majesty to take such steps as may empower a Bishop ' ?

" The Prolocutor.—I am not conscious of what is taking place in the Legislature; but I happen to know that there is a Bill passing through Parliament in reference to the Lectionary, and I cannot help thinking it is desirable to include in it a provision giving liberty to a Bishop to appoint special Psalms for such special occasions as Harvest Thanksgivings.

* " Ascension Day " is here obviously a misprint or mistake—apparently for " The Annunciation."

E

" Archdeacon Clark.—I agree with Prebendary Fagan that it is essential there should be a clear understanding on the matter, and I therefore second his motion for the addition of the words he has suggested.

" Lord A. Compton.—I wish to call attention to the fact that during the last group of Sessions . . . the House was reminded, that at the end of the Lessons appointed for December there is a rubric to the effect, that on any special occasion the Bishop may substitute other Lessons for those appointed in this Calendar, that is, other Lessons than those recommended by the Lectionary Committee; and I think that the same rule may be applied to the Psalms.

" Canon Swainson.—I understand that if I as a clergyman wish to read particular Lessons, I may, with the consent of the Bishop, substitute them; but I do not know that the Bishop has any power to enforce upon me the reading of his substituted Lessons against my will. I maintain that, if this is passed, the Bishop will have no power to enforce the reading of any Psalms upon any clergyman in his diocese.

" The Prolocutor.—Canon Swainson may be certain that whatever rule is applied to the Lessons will be applied to the Psalms.

" The resolution and the rider proposed by Mr. Fagan were then adopted.

" The Prolocutor, accompanied by his assessors, proceeded to the Upper House, and presented to their Lordships the resolution just agreed to by this House. . . . ."—(' Chronicle of Convocation ' (1870), pp. 529–532.)

No answer, that I am aware of, was ever communicated to Convocation—certainly not to the Lower House. The Bill then before Parliament was, as is well known, withdrawn for that Session; and when the new Bill of the following year was brought in, there was, as has already been said, no such provision contained in it.

It is abundantly clear, from these Minutes of the proceedings of the Lower House, that what the House assented to—or understood that it assented to—was the proposal of a power to be given, in the case of the Psalms in like manner as was proposed in the case of the Lessons, to substitute special Psalms on special occasions, with the approval and consent of the Ordinary ; such " special occasions " being Harvest Thanksgivings and the

like; and that, if the power was to include great Festivals of
the Church, the House assented to it only as qualified by an
earnest prayer for such agreement, on the part of the Bishops,
in regard to the Lessons selected, as might secure uniformity in
the several dioceses; and, also, with the understanding that the
freedom of the minister to use the Church's appointed Lessons
would not be taken away.

The "Tables of Lessons Bill," however, having passed in
the Session of 1871, the Bishop of Lincoln held a Diocesan
Synod at Lincoln in the following autumn (Sept. 20, 1871). In
his address delivered in the Synod, after speaking of the new
Lectionary, his Lordship went on to say:

"There is another matter of interest in which we may derive
much benefit from the recent concurrent action of Convocation
and the Legislature in this matter. I refer to the means it affords
us for the additional provision of *special Psalms* and *special
Lessons* for *special occasions.*"

He described it as "a happy thing that appropriate Psalms
may now be sung or said, not merely on some of the great Festivals and Holy Days of the Church, but on *all*. Hitherto," said
the Bishop, "we have sometimes been constrained to use joyful
Psalms on mournful occasions, or mournful Psalms on joyful
ones; but now, by the joint action of Convocation and of Parliament, it has been provided that ' upon occasions to be approved
[appointed, qu.] by the Ordinary, other Psalms may, with his
consent, be substituted for those appointed in the Psalter,' and
this power may be exercised by him on all occasions whereon
' he shall judge that such alteration will conduce to edification.'"
(The Bishop refers, in his published Address, to "the Report of
the Proceedings of Convocation of Canterbury on July 5th and
July 6th, in the ' Chronicle of Convocation ' for 1870, pp. 451
and 530," and to the "Tables of Lessons Act," 34 and 35 Vict.,
chap. 37.) " It is obviously very desirable," the Bishop went
on to say, " that suitable Psalms should be provided for the first
Sunday in Advent "—of which, however, no mention had been
made in Convocation—and so in like manner for the Festival of
the Circumcision, the Epiphany, the Annunciation, Easter Even,
and Trinity Sunday. "This may now be done," said the Bishop.
" Let us thank God for it.

" It is also desirable that a distinct series of Psalms, no less
than of Lessons, should be provided for the use of those who

have three Services in their churches on Sundays. This also is now within our reach.

"The Ordinary is also authorized to permit the substitution on special occasions, such as Harvest Festivals and Church Openings, of appropriate Lessons in lieu of those specified in the Calendar."

"To permit," it is rightly said; for by the wording of the Act, in regard to the Lessons, the Ordinary's function, as before observed, is that of *approval* and *consent*. There appears so far a great increase of liberty. But the Bishop went on to say :

"You will, I am persuaded, my reverend Brethren, concur with me in the opinion, that it is my duty to lose no time in *exercising the authority given to me as Ordinary in this behalf.* After having taken counsel with persons well versed in Liturgical learning, I propose to lay before you to-day a Table of Special Psalms for use on special occasions, and also a series of Psalms for a third service on Sundays and Holy Days, together with an indication of Special Lessons which may be used on certain occasions. ('This portion of the Tables,' it is added in a note, 'is due to the labours of a Committee of the Lower House of Convocation.')"

"Let me commend these Tables to your consideration and use for the next ensuing three years, at the expiration of which they may be revised, if thought necessary." (Address, pp. 17–19.)

Now here at once, from the permissive power accepted by Convocation and sanctioned by the Act, is an exercise of authority precisely that which the Lower House was *not* prepared to recognize ; and the operation of which in different dioceses, with no agreement of the Bishops among themselves, it earnestly prayed might not be introduced, with all the ambiguity which it was apprehensive of, in regard to the nature and extent of these "special occasions." In the "Form and Order of holding the Synod," under the head of "New Lectionary, Additional Proper Psalms, and Proper Lessons on Special Occasions," it is said,

"The Ordinary being *authorized* by the joint action of Parliament and Convocation to *appoint* Special Psalms and Special Lessons on Special Occasions approved by him, the Bishop puts forth in the Synod the following TABLES of Special Psalms and

Special Lessons, which may be used in the Diocese of Lincoln
on occasions therein specified:—

"These TABLES will be subject to revision after the expiration
of three years."

Then follows "Table I. Proper Psalms for Special Occasions,"
including Advent Sunday, the Circumcision, the Epiphany, *the
Purification* [now added], the Annunciation, Thursday before
Easter, Easter Even, Trinity Sunday, the *Festival of St. Michael
and all Angels*, now also added, as well as the "*Days of Apostles
and other Festivals;*" for "*Ember Days*," for "*Rogation Days;*"
as well as "for the Consecration of Churches, or Anniversaries
of their Consecration; and for the reopening of Churches after
Restoration; for the Consecration of Churchyards; for Harvest
Festivals; for School Festivals; for Missionary Services; for
Diocesan Synods, Visitations, or Ruridecanal Chapters."

In the recent Visitation of his Cathedral and Diocese, the
Bishop, in the Second of his Twelve Addresses, thus refers to
the action in this matter already taken in the Diocesan Synod.

"Let me here refer," said his Lordship, "to the 'Table of
PROPER PSALMS AND PROPER LESSONS for certain occasions,'
which was *put forth by the Ordinary* in our Diocesan Synod,
held at Lincoln, September 20th, 1871, for use in this diocese,
under the condition of being subject to revision at the end of
three years."

"Allow me to express a hope that you, my reverend Brethren,
will give effect to these recommendations, and that on Holy Days,
and other times specified therein, you will refer to that 'Table
of Psalms and Lessons,' and avail yourselves of it." (Twelve
Addresses, pp. 55, 56.)

It is given in the Appendix to the Addresses, with consider-
able additions, which, as is stated in a note, had "been put
forth by the Ordinary since the Synod;" *viz.* Psalms for Palm
Sunday, for Monday and Tuesday in Easter Week, Monday and
Tuesday in Whitsun Week, for All Saints' Day, specially; for
St. Matthias' Day; for Choral Festivals, and Benefit Societies.

It might, obviously, admit of an argument whether or not,
in such a case, the order in the Prayer Book applies, *viz.* that
"whensoever Proper Psalms or Lessons are *appointed*, then the
Psalms and Lessons of ordinary course appointed in the Psalter
and Calendar (if they be different) shall be omitted for that

time." But it is easy to see in how very painful a position a
clergyman might find himself placed by a diocesan action
of this kind, under the presumed authority of the Church as
well as of the State; amid circumstances in which he might
feel himself utterly precluded, by considerations of propriety
and duty, from expressing his objections to particular provisions, perhaps deeply affecting, in some cases, his inmost convictions, and practically denying him the liberty which had
seemed to be extended by the supposed "elasticity" of the new
system.

The writer of these notes is convinced that it is quite needless for him to express, how reluctantly he would offer an
opinion at variance with any recommendation or action of one
for whom he entertains so high a respect and so affectionate a
regard as he has for the Bishop of Lincoln. "Amicus Socrates,
amicus Plato, sed magis amica Veritas." And he cannot sup-
press the feeling, that the interests of truth and unity are
deeply involved in the maintenance, among us, of the Book
of Common Prayer, *in its integrity*. It is a bond of union
which, amidst all our differences of opinion and sentiment, still
holds us together as nothing else can; and it would be an irre-
parable loss that we should suffer, if the bond of union were
snapped asunder. Discussions which have lately taken place
will not be without their use, if they have revealed, to the practical conviction of men's minds, how delicate a problem is that
with which we have to deal; and what a flame might be lighted
up, and what elements of discord might be called into existence
and action, by anything like *disintegration* of our Church's order
of ritual and service; holding as it does the balances between
conflicting opinions, apparently irreconcileable as held by ex-
treme parties and rival systems, external to itself, but admitting
perfectly of a true harmony in the view of Christ's one Catholic
Church, in the "one faith" of which they exhibit partial
elements or rays, parted by the prism of sectarian or private
opinion, but which form in their union a pure and perfect
light.

It is obvious to remark that, while the Bishop of Lincoln
adopts for his diocese in such matters the ancient "use of Sarum,"
the Bishop of Salisbury may, in like manner, set himself to
revive in *his* diocese "the use of Lincoln"; the Bishops of North

Wales, with still more evident propriety, if possible, "the use of Bangor," and the Bishops of South Wales "the use of Hereford." And, with yet stronger rights, "the use of York" would claim acceptance in the Northern Province. And thus the intention of our Church at the time of the Reformation would be defeated, and her work undone. Again, not even in the same diocese would there be any uniformity of practice. Inasmuch as on All Saints' Day, by the new Lincoln ordinance, "any of the following [eleven Psalms] may be used" at Matins:—Ps. 1, 11, 15, 16, 20, 30, 33, 34, 61, 79, 84; and at Evensong [eight, *viz.*] Ps. 92, 97, 112, 138, 141, 147, 148, 149, it might easily be that in no two churches of the diocese would the service be the same. In like manner, on days of Apostles, and other festivals, there are fifteen appointed, for the choice of the minister; two having been added to the list put forth at the Synod. There is nothing to prevent Proper Psalms being appointed for every Sunday in the year, and the Prayer Book order thereby entirely superseded. In fact, to the special Psalms for Advent Sunday a note is appended referring to the Table of Psalms appointed for the Third Service on Sundays in Advent; and it is noted, "These may be used also at *Morning Prayer or Evensong on those Sundays.*"

It is, moreover, to be borne in mind that it is not the appointment of "*Proper* Psalms" for "*Special* Occasions" that has been provided for;—a resolution thus worded was distinctly rejected by the Ritual Commission: what was carried was that "upon *occasions*"—any occasions' whatsoever—"*other* Lessons" may "be substituted for those appointed in the Psalter." And this power may be exercised by the Ordinary, as the Bishop of Lincoln observes, "on all occasions whereon" (quoting from the Act) "he shall judge that such alteration will conduce to edification." (It does not appear why this was not printed in the prefatory matter.) On the strength of this provision the Ordinary might, obviously, substitute "other" Psalms for those which contain anything "imprecatory" or "damnatory," if, in his opinion, such alteration would "conduce to edification." As it is worded, the substitution is to be "for those appointed in the *Psalter*"; and therefore, it may be presumed, there would be no power to substitute other Psalms for those appointed in the Table of "Proper Psalms on certain Days." Else there would be another source of danger and mischief opened.

NOTE D.

That which the Archbishop at his Visitation commended to the thoughts of his clergy, I should wish here to recall to mind, was "the duty of carefully considering, in their several spheres, *how far* it was desirable that they should avail themselves of the liberty" now given by the Church, exercising in combined action with the State "the power of adapting her services to the wants of her children;" and in particular, in reference to "opportunities of Common Prayer" opened to him, "which were denied to him before." To this question it seemed to me specially fitting that I should apply myself, with a view to rendering such assistance as I might, in my office, to the clergy in the practical consideration of this question. In connection with this subject I have great satisfaction in quoting, as I do with entire concurrence, an expression of opinion from the Bishop of Lincoln, contained in the Visitation Address, already referred to, in the way of a caution to his clergy as to the expediency of their availing themselves, in another respect, of the liberty of abridgment now permitted by the law. The Bishop says,—

"It is the office of the Church of God to guard and authenticate and preach God's word, and she does this by the public reading of Scripture, which is the best preaching. Until last year, for more than three centuries it was the glory of the Church of England, among the churches of Christendom, that not a day passed but she read four chapters of Holy Scripture. But in an evil hour (as I presume to think), in a hurried Session of the Convocation of the province, on February 13th, it was agreed that, on almost all week-days throughout the year, the officiating minister in a parish church may be at liberty to *omit one Lesson* at Morning Prayer and one at Evening Prayer; and this permission was afterwards authorized by the Legislature, although, by the NEW LECTIONARY, sanctioned in the preceding year, 1871, the Scripture Lessons had been much curtailed; so that, unless we decline to use this permission, our people are now to be content with the stinted allowance of two short Lessons daily, whereas formerly they had the benefit of four longer ones.

"Let me, therefore, express an earnest hope, my reverend Brethren, that no clergyman in this diocese will avail himself of this permission, but will read two Lessons at Matins and Even-song. It was the practice of the primitive Church to read both Testaments together. If you begin to disparage the Old Testament, as compared with the New, or to contrast one Testament with the other, and to weigh one against the other in the opposite scale of human opinion, we shall soon lose both Testaments. 'What God hath joined together, let not man put asunder.'" (Twelve Addresses, pp. 51–53.)

In the same sense the Archdeacon of Buckingham, the Pro-locutor of the Lower House of Convocation, in his Visitation Charge of the present year, says,—

"With regard to the Shortened Service, I would venture to express my hope that advantage may not be too freely taken of the liberty granted by the Act to omit one of the Lessons. I am not finding fault with a relaxation which may occasionally be found convenient; but I cannot forget that it was the practice of the early Church to read both Testaments together; and it would be, in my judgment, a serious loss, as well as a grave departure from primitive usage, if the habit were to become general, of reading one Lesson only at our Daily Morning and Evening Prayer." (Charge, p. 28.)

In connection with this subject, of the reading of Holy Scripture in the Church, I cannot refrain from continuing the quotation from the Lincoln Visitation Address. "That we have gained much by the New Table of Lessons," the Bishop of Lincoln thinks, "we must thankfully acknowledge; but that we have also lost a great deal," he freely admits and plainly expresses, "we must no less sorrowfully deplore. The use of the New Lectionary for more than a year," says the Bishop, "has now discovered many blemishes and defects in it to the careful students of Scripture. It is much to be wished that the use of the New Table had been made provisional. And let me here offer a suggestion," the Bishop adds, "that the term fixed in the 'Table of Lessons Act' for the final *abandonment* of the *Old* Lectionary, namely, January 1, 1879, should also be made an occasion for the *revision* of the *New* Table of Lessons." (Second Address, p. 53.)

If any further Rubrical revision be taken in hand, the first subject in order for consideration and revisal would be in the prefatory matter to the Book of Common Prayer, "The order how the rest of Holy Scripture is appointed to be read," and with it the whole question of the appointed order of reading Holy Scripture in the Church, specially in regard to the Sunday Lessons. Part of this prefatory matter, as it is given in our Prayer Books lately printed, rests entirely upon the authority of the *Queen's Printers*, with a warrant of some sort given by the Ritual Commission in communication with the Government. It appears that at one of the last meetings of the Commission (the 104th), held May 17, 1870,

"The Secretary read a communication from the Queen's Printers, suggesting that some alteration was necessary in the preface directing how the rest of Holy Scripture is appointed to be read, in order to *adapt* it to the new Lectionary, *as being now reprinted*, for the purposes of a Bill before Parliament."

Thereupon it was moved and seconded, " and agreed, *nemine contradicente*, that the Chairman be requested to address a communication to the head of Her Majesty's Government, suggesting that the Queen's Printer be authorized, under the circumstances, to print the paragraph as amended by the Commission at its last meeting." (Report, pp. 123, 124.)

No further notice appears as to whether such communication was made, or whether any or what reply was made to it.

The Minute in regard to the amended paragraph referred to, as agreed upon at the preceding meeting, stands thus :—

" The Bishop of Chester moved, and Earl Beauchamp seconded, and it was agreed, *nemine contradicente*, that the second paragraph in the preface, setting forth how the rest of Holy Scripture is appointed to be read, be amended as follows :—

" ' *The New Testament is appointed for the Second Lessons at Morning and Evening Prayer, and shall be read over orderly every year twice, besides the Epistles and Gospels, except the Apocalypse, which shall be read once in addition to certain proper Lessons appointed upon divers Feasts.*' " (Report, p. 123.)

A somewhat remarkable circumstance, however, is that the Queen's Printers did *not* so print it. They discovered, probably, that " *the* Apocalypse " was *not* ordered to be read as a whole, three chapters being omitted (*viz.* the 9th, 13th, and 18th) ; and consequently they printed the last clause as it had stood before, with a new insertion, thus:—"except the Apocalypse, out of which there are only [*certain Lessons appointed at the end of the year, and*] certain Proper Lessons appointed upon divers Feasts," —the portion here enclosed within brackets being inserted. But there was no action, as might have been expected, of the Ritual Commission to supply the omission which the Queen's Printers had pointed out ; and when at the last meeting of all (the 108th), held June 28, 1870, the committee that had been appointed " reported their amendment of the Schedule " to be appended to the Fourth Report, we find—

" Earl Beauchamp then asked leave to insert certain paragraphs in the First Schedule, in lieu of the amended ' Order how the rest of Holy Scripture is appointed to be read,' so as to adapt them, with an amendment, to the Bill now before Parliament on the new Table of Lessons ; but after a division the motion was, by leave, withdrawn." (Report, p. 129.)

Meanwhile the Queen's Printers made the important change of " twice " for "thrice " in regard to the reading of the New Testament. " The New Testament is appointed for the Second Lessons at Morning and Evening Prayer, and shall be read over orderly every year *twice*, once in the morning and once in the evening, besides the Epistles and Gospels, except the Apocalypse," &c. So it stands printed : but Her Majesty's Printers had no lawful authority given them to declare this to be the order of the Church of England. Indeed, the present order of the Church and the State, while there is the option left of reading either the old Tables of Lessons or the new, is, in fact, that the New Testament shall be read over orderly every year *thrice*, or otherwise (if the new Lessons are read) *twice*. It is, in fact, though not a " provisional " use that has been allowed by the Act, an *alternative*, or *optional* use ; if only the Act be left free and unfettered in its provisions.

While these pages have been passing through the press, there has appeared (in the ' Guardian,' Sept. 3, 1873) a report of the proceedings at the Annual Conference in the Diocese of Carlisle, held on August 19th and 20th. Under the head of the " Act of Uniformity Amendment Act," the Bishop said, the point which he had chiefly in mind when he proposed this question—" What useful application can be made in the diocese of Carlisle of this Act?"—was that which was touched by ten deaneries in the following suggestion, " The more general adoption of daily or more frequent week-day services." " I was anxious," said the Bishop, " to elicit opinion as to the practicability and consequent propriety of opening our churches more frequently to divine worship, under the condition of using a shorter service than that prescribed by the Book of Common Prayer. In many churches of this mountain diocese I conceive that it is impossible to make a week-day service really profitable for edification. There are, probably, many of which this can be said, and which nevertheless are shut up except on the first day of the week. I feel myself therefore emboldened, by the expressed opinions of meetings which may be said to represent half the diocese, to urge the consideration, whether it might not be desirable to open many of our churches on week-days, either morning or evening, as circumstances may dictate, for a short service of prayer, with or without an exposition or a sermon. I may add that I believe the chief value of this Act is with reference to week-day and special services. So far as the accustomed worship of Sunday is concerned, it will be found that the chief value of the Act is to give legal sanction to certain arrangements, which convenience had dictated, but the legality of which was regarded as doubtful. I venture to express my hope that the powers of the Act will be sparingly applied in changing the custom of the parishes with regard to Sunday service ; I feel a little afraid lest the rigid uniformity of past years should be replaced by too great a love of variety. I confess, for example, that I should regard with sorrow the omission of the Litany from our morning service ; and I should specially grieve over its absence when the Holy Communion was to be administered. Writers on liturgical questions tell us that it is the most suitable introduction to that solemn service, and my own feelings certainly assent to their decision."

Before the close of the Conference, to meet, as it would appear, some misapprehension of what he had expressed, the Bishop took occasion to say that, in regard to the Litany, " all he said was this, that the best writers tell us the Litany was the proper introduction to the Holy Communion, and so far as his own feelings went he agreed with that ; but he did not wish, as Bishop, to interfere with the freedom of the clergy in this matter. Regarding generally the question of morning services, the advice he would give was that each clergyman should consider what was best for his own parish, and do it. Now they had got further liberty under this Act, he urged them not to avail themselves too readily of it, but rather to take a conservative view of the powers it gave them."

NOTE E.

It is hardly necessary to record here, that the Report of the Joint Committee, agreed upon in Lambeth in December last, with the Report of the Special Committee of the Lower House, having been adopted, with certain amendments by the Lower House in the February sessions, was taken into consideration by the Upper House, in the May sessions, and with the amendments made by their Lordships, was considered again by the Lower House, and finally assented to on the last day of that group of sessions. Looking to the general expression of opinion there, and also in the great body of the clergy throughout the country, and still more, of the Church laity, testified especially by the feeling shown in so remarkable a manner in the great meeting held in London on the 31st of January, it may be safely said, without much doubt, in the language of the Venerable the Prolocutor, in his recent Charge to the Clergy of his archdeaconry, that " the removal of the Athanasian Creed from our Service Book is not an event at all likely to come to pass in this nineteenth century."

An organ of public opinion, sensitively alive to the " popularis aura," and not likely to exaggerate the dangers of expansiveness and elasticity of creeds and formularies, said very significantly, not very long ago, in words worthy to be borne in mind, and practically acted upon :—

" A very great danger for the Church lurks in the very comprehensiveness which is her boast. The strength of other sects and communions lies in the definiteness and rigour with which they are prepared to face the problems of religious life. It remains to be proved whether the Church of England, without forfeiting the breadth of which she is justly proud, can hold her own in this vigorous struggle of positive creeds." There had been claimed for her " no less energy in the assertion of positive truth than in the maintenance of open questions. There is no danger of her failing in the latter point "—was the sagacious comment of the spokesman of public opinion—" *but her best friends may well be anxious about the former.*"

May it be her blessedness to have it said of her, by the gracious voice of Him " who walketh in the midst of the seven golden candlesticks," " Thou hast a little strength, and hast kept my word, and not denied my name." And may this be her portion and privilege, "Because thou hast kept the word of my patience, I also will keep thee from the hour of temptation, which shall come upon all the world, to try them that dwell upon the earth." And, in order thereto, may she never forget the warning, by that loving yet awful Voice, "Behold, I come quickly: hold that fast which thou hast, that no man take thy crown." (Rev. iii. 8, 10, 11.)

NOTE F.

It cannot be too clearly or too generally understood, that the only solution of the problem which the advocates of "Disestablishment and Disendowment" propose to themselves is, the essential "Secularization," entire "Desecration" of the Church, its patrimony, its fabrics, and everything that belongs to it. The last scheme which had fallen in the way of the writer, when he was holding his Visitation, was propounded in 'Macmillan's Magazine' for April last, in an article entitled "Disestablishment and Disendowment, with a proposal for a really National Church of England," by Alfred R. Wallace, F.R.S. The article is introduced by a note of the editor's, expressing that, whether the views set forth in it "can ever be realized in detail or not, it is certainly most desirable that the doctrine, that 'Church property of every kind is national property, to be secured,' as Arnold expressed it, 'for ever for public use, something saved out of the scramble, which no covetousness can appropriate and no folly waste,' should be put forward in strong and uncompromising terms by an able and eminent man of science like Mr. Wallace, even though the particular mode he proposes of carrying the doctrine into practice may seem to some inadequate or even problematical."

The writer of the article desiderates some "practicable and beneficial mode of applying the national property now held by the Church, or of preserving and *utilizing* for *national objects* the *parish churches* and other ecclesiastical buildings spread so thickly over our land, and which constitute a picturesque and impressive record of much of our social and religious history for nearly a thousand years." "The main principle," he lays down, "that should guide our action in this matter," as he conceives, is "that existing Church property of every kind is national pro-

perty, and that no portion of it must under any circumstances
be alienated, either for the compensation of supposed or real
vested interests, or to the use of any sectarian body ; and further,
that *the parish churches* and other ecclesiastical buildings must
on no account be given up, but be permanently retained, *with the
Church property,* for analogous purposes to those for which they
were primarily established—the *moral and social advancement* of
the whole community."

" It must, I think," says Mr. Wallace, " be admitted that an
institution which provides for the residence in every parish of
the kingdom of a permanent representative of the best morality
and culture of the age—a man whose first duty it is to be the
friend of all who are in trouble, who lives an unselfish life,
devoting himself to the moral and physical improvement of the
community, who is a welcome visitor to every house, who keeps
free from all party strife and personal competition, and who, by
his education and training, can efficiently promote all sanitary
measures and healthful amusements, and show by his example
the beauty of a true and virtuous life—that an institution which
should really do this, would constitute an educational machinery,
whose influence on the true advancement of society can hardly
be exaggerated. But" then, it would appear, "in order that
such an organization should produce the full beneficial effect of
what it is capable, it is above all things essential that it should
keep itself free from *sectarian teaching,* and from everything calcu-
lated to exert *religious prejudices.*" There must be no "adoption
of a *fixed creed* by the Established Church."

The writer of the article accordingly proceeds to sketch out
what he considers " should be the status and duties of the man
who will *take the place of the existing clergyman* as the head and
representative in every parish and district of the National
Church.

" First, as to his designation ; he might be termed the rector, a
name to which we are already accustomed, and which *does not neces-
sarily imply a religious teacher.* He should be chosen, primarily,
for moral, intellectual, and social qualities, of a much higher
character than are now expected." Among other things, it
appears, "he should be specially trained in the *laws of health*
and their practical application, and in the principles of *the most
advanced political and social economy.* His religion should be
quite free from *sectarian prejudices,* but his private opinions on

religious matters would be no subject for inquiry. He should, however, be of *a religious frame of mind*, so as to be able to work sympathetically with the clergy of the various religious bodies in his district, and excite in them *neither distrust nor antagonism.* He must have a fair knowledge of *physiology*, and of *simple medicine and surgery*, of the rudiments of *law* and *legal procedure*, of the principles of *scientific agriculture*, and of the *natural-history sciences*, as well as whatever is considered essential to the education of a cultivated man."

"The duties of the parish rector would comprise, among others, all those of the existing clergyman; *but he would never conduct religious services of any kind (sic, ital.).* The *parish church*, with its appurtenances, would, however, be under his entire authority, in trust for the whole body of parishioners, to be used for religious services by all or any duly organized religious bodies, under such arrangements as he might find to be most convenient for all. Any religious body should be able to claim the use of the church as a right (subject to the equal rights of all other bodies); the only condition being that it should possess a permanent organization, and that its ministers should be an *educated class* of men, coming up to a certain standard of *intellectual* culture and moral character."

" The rector would himself *lecture* in *the church* on *moral, social, sanitary, historical, philosophical*, or *any other topics* which he judged most suitable to the circumstances of his parishioners. He would also allow the church to be used during the week for any purpose not inconsistent with the main objects of his position. His knowledge of law, and his position as *ex-officio* magistrate, would enable him to settle almost all the petty disputes among his parishioners, and so, greatly diminish lawsuits. He would be an *ex-officio* member of the School Board, and of the governing body of any other public educational institution in his district. It would be his duty to see that new legislative enactments were brought to the notice of the persons they chiefly affected, so that no one could offend through ignorance. He might, *if he pleased*, visit the sick, if his services were asked for, but this would be altogether voluntary. It would be an essential part of his duty to be on good terms with the ministers of all religious sects in his district, to bring them into friendly relations with each other, and to induce them to work harmoniously together for moral and educational objects."

" Of course there would be some high officers fulfilling the duties of bishops, or inspectors over the rectors; and over the whole a Supreme Board, or a Minister of Public Instruction ; but these are matters which would offer no difficulty in an institution of which the main features are so well marked out." ('Macmillan's Magazine,' No. 162, pp. 498–503.)

The writer of this article, it must be allowed, has done some service in attempting fairly to embody in an actual form the theory, which is the only approved one in the present day, among the friends of " disestablishment and disendowment," *viz.* the application, to all things hitherto regarded as sacred, of the process of utilization and secularization, on principles undenominational, non-religious, and therefore, in the fullest sense of the term, irreligious. We know that, on the principles of *physical* hydrostatics, water will not rise above its level ; and it is simply impossible, in the philosophy of the *moral* world, that that which springs from a source which is of the earth, earthy, can produce results which are from above, derived from the supernal fountain of things heavenly. There can be but one result. The experiment was tried by a nation of old; and this was the verdict pronounced upon it, and proved by bitter experience to be true. " For my people have committed two evils ; they have forsaken me the fountain of living waters, and hewed them out cisterns, broken cisterns, that can hold no water" (Jer. ii. 13). The secularized "rector," and his desecrated parsonage, will be looked to in vain for even the temporal and social benefits and blessings to the people around him, of which "the village preacher's modest mansion" was once the home and centre. Our churches, no doubt, would, many of them, be excellent lecture-halls, and grand concert-rooms; but it is earnestly to be hoped Churchmen will do nothing, in a would-be "utilizing" of sacred buildings, to pave the way for utter desecration and degradation.

The exclusion of the religious, or as it is called now-a-days the " denominational " or " sectarian " element, must infallibly exclude any effective inculcation even of the *moral* lessons which in modern systems are to be all in all. " Let all bitterness, and wrath, and anger, and clamour, and evil speaking, be put away from you, with all malice : and be ye kind one to another, tender-hearted, forgiving one another " — this is the lesson

F

which patrons of British and Foreign schools, " Unsectarian," and even Secular schools, would wish to teach—but where is to be found the *motive*, or the example ? Not where the Apostle found it—" *even as God for Christ's sake hath forgiven you. Be ye* THEREFORE *followers of God*, as dear children ; and walk in love, as Christ also hath loved us "—here is the same motive, the same example come in again—" as Christ also hath loved us, and hath *given himself for us an offering and a sacrifice to God for a sweet-smelling savour.*" (Eph. iv. 31, 32 ; v. 1, 2.) We are here at once—and on Christian principles, and the principles of human nature, inevitably—in the very midst of " dogma," the very deepest, inward mysteries of Christian Faith. Divine Wisdom has long ago set before us the choice—the only choice we have. " Either make the tree good and his fruit good," said our Blessed Lord ; " or else make the tree corrupt, and his fruit corrupt: for the tree is known by his fruit." " For of thorns men do not gather figs, nor of a bramble bush gather they grapes." (S. Matt. xii. 33 ; S. Luke, vi. 44.)

BY THE SAME AUTHOR.

Recently Published.

CHARGE, 1871.

Visitation Courts and Synods. A Charge
delivered to the Clergy of the Archdeaconry of Maidstone,
at the Ordinary Visitation in May, 1871.   Price 1*s.*

The Unity of a Christian Kingdom in the
One Church of God.   A Sermon preached in Canterbury
Cathedral, February 27, 1872, being the Day of National
Thanksgiving to Almighty God for the Recovery of H.R.H.
Albert Edward, Prince of Wales.   Price 1*s.*

www.ingramcontent.com/pod-product-compliance
Lightning Source LLC
Chambersburg PA
CBHW021518090426
42739CB00007B/673